Ripley Readers

Caves!

All true and unbelievable!

Ripley
PUBLISHING
a Jim Pattison Company

Hello in there! This cave is dark and deep!

Ripley Readers

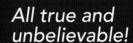

All true and unbelievable!

Learning to read. Reading to learn!

DEC 0 7 2020

LEVEL ONE Sounding It Out Preschool–Kindergarten
For kids who know their alphabet and are starting to sound out words.

learning sight words • beginning reading • sounding out words

LEVEL TWO Reading with Help Preschool–Grade 1
For kids who know sight words and are learning to sound out new words.

expanding vocabulary • building confidence • sounding out bigger words

LEVEL THREE Independent Reading Grades 1-3
For kids who are beginning to read on their own.

introducing paragraphs • challenging vocabulary • reading for comprehension

LEVEL FOUR Chapters Grades 2–4
For confident readers who enjoy a mixture of images and story.

reading for learning • more complex content • feeding curiosity

Ripley Readers Designed to help kids build their reading skills and confidence at any level, this program offers a variety of fun, entertaining, and unbelievable topics to interest even the most reluctant readers. With stories and information that will spark their curiosity, each book will motivate them to start and keep reading.

PUBLISHING

Vice President, Licensing & Publishing Amanda Joiner
Editorial Manager Carrie Bolin

Editor Jordie R. Orlando
Writer Korynn Wible-Freels
Designer Scott Swanson
Reprographics Bob Prohaska
Production Design Luis Fuentes

Published by Ripley Publishing 2020

10 9 8 7 6 5 4 3 2 1

Copyright © 2020 Ripley Publishing

ISBN: 978-1-60991-406-6

Email: publishing@ripleys.com
www.ripleys.com/books
Manufactured in China in May 2020.

First Printing

Library of Congress Control Number:
2020937128

For more information regarding permission,
contact:
VP Licensing & Publishing
Ripley Entertainment Inc.
7576 Kingspointe Parkway, Suite 188
Orlando, Florida 32819

PUBLISHER'S NOTE
While every effort has been made to verify
the accuracy of the entries in this book, the
Publisher cannot be held responsible for any
errors contained in the work. They would be
glad to receive any information from readers.

PHOTO CREDITS

Cover © salajean/Shutterstock **Master Graphics** Created by Scott Swanson **3** © salajean/Shutterstock
4-5 David Díez Barrio/Getty Images **6** Francesco Riccardo Iacomino/Getty Images **7** Westend61/Getty
Images **8-9** krisanapong detraphiphat/Getty Images **10-11** Phuvich Chavitrutaigul/Getty Images
12-13 Jonathan Irish/Getty Images **14-15** Olivier Parent/Alamy Stock Photo **16** Mike Kemp/In Pictures via
Getty Images **17** milehightraveler/Getty Images **18-19** Nathan L Roker/Getty Images **20-21** Pakin Songmor/
Getty Images **22-23** © Vladimir Wrangel/Shutterstock **24-25** Nature Picture Library/Alamy Stock Photo
26-27 Matteo Colombo/Getty Images **28-29** CARSTEN PETER/SPELEORESEARCH & FILMS/National
Geographic Image Collection **30-31** Henrik Sorensen/Getty Images

All other photos are from Ripley Entertainment Inc. Every attempt has been made to acknowledge correctly
and contact copyright holders and we apologize in advance for any unintentional errors or omissions, which
will be corrected in future editions.

A cave is a hole in a hill
or under the ground.

Caves are all over the world, from mountain tops to under the water.

You can find them where it is hot, cold, sunny, or snowy.

Water, wind, and moving rocks break down stone to make caves.

Lava and ice can make them, too!

Caves are very old and
take many years to form.

Some caves were around with the dinosaurs!

A cave is like a maze in the earth!

This one goes on for miles. Do you think you could find the end?

When mineral water drips from the top of a cave, it makes a stalactite.

They come in a lot of shapes.
These are called soda straws!

When minerals pile up on the ground, they make a stalagmite.

They can be big or small. Some of them are taller than you!

Why can't your eyes
see in a cave?

There is no light! It is
too dark!

Some caves are so deep that
a skyscraper could fit in them!

Want to know something cool?

Blind cavefish do not have eyes!
Caves are so dark they don't
need them!

Did you know that bats are not really blind?

This cave is home to
twenty million of them!

Blue and green glow worms can light up a cave!

Just look at how pretty they are!

Some of the white crystals in this cave are as long as a school bus!

Going into a cave is called spelunking.

Do you want to explore a cave someday?